OLYMPIC HOT STREAKS

BY RYAN WILLIAMSON

MOMENTUM

Published by The Child's World®
1980 Lookout Drive • Mankato, MN 56003-1705
800-599-READ • www.childsworld.com

Photographs ©: Melissa J. Perenson/Cal Sports
Media/AP Images, cover, 1; Leonard Zhukovsky/
Shutterstock Images, 5, 26, 28; AP Images, 6, 8,
9; Dieter Endlicher/AP Images, 10; Eric Risberg/AP
Images, 12; Katsumi Kasahara/AP Images, 14, 16;
Elaine Thompson/AP Images, 18; Al Behrman/AP
Images, 21; Mark Baker/AP Images, 22; Red Line
Editorial, 25

ISBN 9781503832336
LCCN 2018963098

Printed in the United States of America
PA02422

ABOUT THE AUTHOR

Ryan Williamson is a sportswriter based in the Minneapolis–Saint Paul area. He has written articles that have appeared in various publications across the country. He graduated from the University of Missouri with a degree in print/digital sports journalism.

CONTENTS

FAST FACTS 4

CHAPTER ONE
Heiden Skates to Gold **7**

CHAPTER TWO
Joyner's Record Runs **11**

CHAPTER THREE
A Wrestling Upset **15**

CHAPTER FOUR
Team USA's Softball Gold **19**

CHAPTER FIVE
Phelps Strikes Gold **23**

CHAPTER SIX
Biles's Rio Performance **27**

Think About It 29
Glossary 30
Source Notes 31
To Learn More 32
Index 32

MOMENTUM

FAST FACTS

The Olympic Games
► There are both Summer and Winter Olympic Games. The first modern Summer Olympics took place in Greece in 1896. Athletes from 14 different countries participated. The first Winter Olympics took place in 1924 in Chamonix, France.

Who Is Competing?
► Athletes from countries around the world compete in the Olympics. They wear uniforms that show which country they are from.

► Athletes compete in either individual or team events.

Different Sports
► Different sports are featured during the Summer and Winter Olympics. The Summer Olympics has sports such as swimming, track and field, gymnastics, and volleyball. All winter sports involve snow or ice. Figure skating, ice hockey, and skiing are all Winter Olympic sports.

**Athletes from the United States participated ►
in the Olympic opening ceremony in 2018.**

CHAPTER ONE

HEIDEN SKATES TO GOLD

Eric Heiden, who was born in Wisconsin, could see his breath as he stood on the ice rink. He skated toward the starting line of the 500-meter speed skating finals. This was his first chance to win a gold medal at the 1980 Winter Olympics in Lake Placid, New York. He took his place and prepared himself. Then the gun went off to signal the start of the race. Heiden knew he would need to perform at his best to beat his opponent, Yevgeny Kulikov of the Soviet Union.

The two racers started quickly. They swung their arms, took long **strides**, and stayed neck and neck as they skated around the track. As they raced to the first turn, Kulikov picked up speed. He **glided** ahead and slowly built his lead over Heiden. Kulikov used the next few meters to build an even bigger lead. Heiden needed to catch up in the next turn.

◄ **Eric Heiden was the first person to win all five speed skating events in one Olympics.**

▲ **Heiden started speed skating seriously when he was 14 years old. He trained five hours every day.**

Heiden turned quickly and kept his balance. He was just a step or two behind Kulikov. The finish line was near. But Heiden saw his chance to skate ahead and redoubled his efforts. He pushed his arms from side to side as he tried to pick up speed any way he could. As they approached the finish line, Heiden continued to speed up. Kulikov, meanwhile, ran out of energy. He could only watch as Heiden easily crossed the finish line first.

▲ **Heiden (center) made Olympic history after winning his fifth gold medal.**

Though he had just set an Olympic record at 38.03 seconds and had won a gold medal, Heiden didn't show much emotion. He flipped off his hood and skated around as U.S. fans in the stands cheered loudly in the brisk winter air. After the 500-meter speed skating finals, Heiden went on to skate past the competition in three more races, winning gold in each.

Heiden's final event was the 10,000-meter race. Heiden skated around the ice and eventually finished with another world record. This time there was a smile on his face. Heiden had won five gold medals. That had never been done before at the Winter Olympics.

CHAPTER TWO

JOYNER'S RECORD RUNS

Florence Griffith Joyner stared down the track with her hands on her hips. She was ready for the finals of the 100-meter dash at the 1988 Summer Olympics in Seoul, South Korea. When the race began, Griffith Joyner didn't stand out. She was in the third spot on the track, racing right alongside her competition. But then Griffith Joyner found an extra burst of speed. She could feel her heart pounding quickly in her chest. Suddenly, she was ahead.

The finish line was getting closer and closer. Griffith Joyner picked up the pace as she began to take a wide lead. Her long strides made her nearly impossible to beat. Within a matter of three seconds, Griffith Joyner had gone from running with the pack to leading the race. She crossed the finish line. Her hands were up in the air. She knew she was a gold medalist.

◄ **Florence Griffith Joyner competed in both the 1984 and 1988 Olympics. She won a total of three gold medals and two silver medals.**

▲ **Griffith Joyner waves to a cheering crowd after winning a gold medal.**

Her hands stayed in the air as she continued running down the track. Eventually, a teammate brought her a U.S. flag to wave. She was enjoying her moment of victory.

After the 100-meter dash came the 200-meter race. Once again, the sprinter nicknamed "Flo-Jo" stayed with the pack early in the race.[1] Then she unleashed a burst of speed. Once again, she crossed the finish line first. She had set the world record by running the race in 21.34 seconds. The previous world record was 21.56 seconds. As the U.S. national anthem played to celebrate her win, tears of joy streamed down Griffith Joyner's face. And yet her amazing run was not yet over. Before the Games were finished, Flo-Jo won another gold medal in the 4x100-meter **relay** and a silver medal in the 4x200 relay. Even today, fans still speak of her dominant 1988 Olympics.

A RECORD-SETTING HEPTATHLON

Another person emerged as a star at the 1988 Summer Olympics: Jackie Joyner-Kersee. Her brother, Al Joyner, was married to Florence Griffith Joyner. Joyner-Kersee competed in the **heptathlon**. Coming in, she had already set the world record for overall score with 7,215 points when qualifying for the 1988 Olympics. Her best events were the long jump, 100-meter hurdles, 200-meter run, and high jump. Once Joyner-Kersee got to the Games, she put on a remarkable performance. She broke her previous record with 7,291 points.

CHAPTER THREE

A WRESTLING UPSET

Wrestler Rulon Gardner of the United States stepped onto the mat. He stood next to his opponent, Russian **heavyweight** Aleksandr Karelin. Gardner had never won a medal while representing his country. He had a large **frame** and looked like a strong wrestler, but he did not have much of a reputation. But Gardner had captured U.S. fans' attention once he won his first four matches to get to the final.

Meanwhile, Karelin was large and fearsome. He was going for his fourth **consecutive** Olympic gold medal. To complete his amazing run, Gardner would have to beat one of the sport's all-time greats. But he wasn't fazed. He waited for the referee to start this gold medal match at the 2000 Summer Olympics in Sydney, Australia. The next several minutes changed Gardner's life forever.

◄ **Few people expected Rulon Gardner (right) to beat Aleksandr Karelin.**

▲ Gardner started wrestling when he was six years old.

Early on in the match, the two wrestlers stood holding each other up with their hands locked together. Each made sure his opponent couldn't move and score any points. The two stood in the same position for three minutes until the first period ended.

This deadlock continued until the second period. Gardner finally broke the 0–0 tie when Karelin's hands came apart. This allowed Gardner to take the 1–0 lead. During the next few minutes, Karelin tried to get Gardner down. But the dairy farmer from Wyoming wouldn't budge. His big frame helped him keep his position.

In international wrestling, a match automatically goes to overtime unless the winner has at least three points. The score was still only 1–0, so the match headed into a three-minute overtime. Fans held their breath. Fans of Gardner and Team USA stood, trying to encourage Gardner to hold on. U.S. flags in the crowd waved wildly as Gardner kept Karelin from scoring.

As the final few seconds ticked off the clock, Karelin started to slowly give up. He knew he couldn't win. The crowd began to roar as time ran out. The referee soon grabbed Gardner's hand and quickly lifted it up to signal that he had won the gold. Gardner kept his cool with just a smile. To cap off his amazing performance in Sydney, he became the first wrestler to knock off Karelin in more than a decade.

CHAPTER FOUR

TEAM USA'S SOFTBALL GOLD

The softball game had just started. But Team USA looked as if it was already in trouble against Australia. It was the first inning and the score was 0–0. Australia had two runners on base and was looking to take the lead. Players from both teams had intense looks on their faces. The two teams and their fans were loudly cheering, hoping to gain an edge.

The United States had dominated its competition throughout the 2004 Summer Olympics in Athens, Greece. Through eight games, the United States had won. No opponent had so much as scored against the Americans. Now, Team USA just had to complete its dominant performance by beating Australia. A win would secure the Team USA's third gold medal in a row in softball.

◀ **Lisa Fernandez has three gold medals. She won them in 1996, 2000, and 2004.**

U.S. pitcher Lisa Fernandez wasn't worried about the two runners on bases. She used her decade of experience on the mound to stay focused. She could feel support from her friends and family in the stands.

Fernandez looked at each batter and intimidated them with her fast pitches. Hitters left the batter's box frustrated over and over again. Finally, an Australian batter grounded out and ended the inning without a run.

Team USA had hit well all tournament. The players knew third baseman Crystl Bustos could hit a home run at any time. In the first inning, she hit the ball hard. It soared high in the air and flew down the field. The Australian center fielder stayed in her spot as she watched the ball sail over the fence. A few innings later, Bustos hit another long home run. Then, catcher Stacey Nuveman got one, too. The United States was ahead 5–0.

At the top of the seventh inning, it was Australia's final chance to come back. Team USA was ahead 5–1. Fernandez took a deep breath and fired the pitch from where she stood in the middle of the diamond. The batter hit a ball to a U.S. infielder. She threw it to first base. It was the third out, and the game was over. Team USA had won. The U.S. players threw their gloves into the air in celebration as soon as the out was recorded.

**Team USA celebrates with each other on ▶
the field after beating Australia.**

CHAPTER FIVE

PHELPS STRIKES GOLD

Michael Phelps could only stand and watch as his teammates swam the length of the Olympic pool. Water dripped down his face. Phelps was a U.S. swimmer, and he had already swum his part of the 4x100-meter **freestyle** relay race.

Phelps was out to make history in the 2008 Summer Olympic Games in Beijing, China. His goal was to win eight gold medals. No one had ever won more than seven gold medals in one Olympics. The freestyle relay would bring Phelps his second gold medal in 2008. For the freestyle competition, Phelps was the first U.S. swimmer to enter the pool.

Once Phelps was done, he watched other countries' swimmers pull ahead of his U.S. teammates. But the whole time, Phelps cheered. "You could tell I was pretty excited," Phelps said. "I lost my voice and I was definitely pretty emotional out there."[2]

◄ **Brendan Hansen, Aaron Peirsol, and Michael Phelps watch in anticipation as their teammate Jason Lezak competes in the medley relay.**

Jason Lezak was the final U.S. swimmer in the relay. He trailed the leader of the race and needed to catch up to help his team win gold and keep Phelps's streak alive. The U.S. swimmer swam as fast as he could. He was slowly starting to catch up.

As millions of people watched, Team USA drew closer and closer to coming back for the win. As the U.S. and French teams approached the finish, the swimmers for both teams stood waiting to see who would touch the wall first. When the finish came, Team USA had won by less than one second. The U.S. swimmers began a wild celebration. The team had won the gold. "Jason finished that race better than we could even ask for," Phelps later said.[3] His run for eight gold medals continued.

Phelps won gold medal after gold medal. Phelps's final gold medal race came in another relay: the 4x100-meter medley race. He already had seven gold medals. Phelps entered the water as the third of a four-man relay. Swimming the butterfly, his arms smacked the water violently with each stroke. That approach allowed Phelps to pass two teams and put the United States in the lead heading into the final part of the relay.

Lezak was the closer again. He finished the race strong. His fingers touched the wall shortly before the next closest team. Phelps stood as close as he could to see when Lezak's fingers touched.

When Phelps saw that his team had won, he immediately screamed and put his index finger in the air. It was official. Phelps finished off the ultimate hot streak with his eighth gold medal in the 2008 Olympics.

U.S. OLYMPIANS WITH THE MOST MEDALS

NAME	EVENT	MEDALS			TOTAL
Michael Phelps	Swimming	23	3	2	28
Ryan Lochte	Swimming	6	3	3	12
Natalie Coughlin	Swimming	3	4	5	12
Jenny Thompson	Swimming	8	3	1	12
Dara Torres	Swimming	4	4	4	12
Matt Biondi	Swimming	8	2	1	11
Carl Osburn	Shooting	5	4	2	11
Mark Spitz	Swimming	9	1	1	11
Gary Hall Jr.	Swimming	5	3	2	10
Carl Lewis	Track & Field	9	1		10

CHAPTER SIX

BILES'S RIO PERFORMANCE

Simone Biles stood on the gymnasium floor with a serious look on her face. She was about to begin her floor exercise routine in the team gymnastics competition at the 2016 Summer Olympics. The Games were taking place in Rio de Janeiro, Brazil. The crowd sat quietly, waiting to see what was about to happen.

When the music began to play, all eyes were on Biles. She glided around the floor and leaped into the air. Then she ran across the floor and nailed her flips. The crowd roared in approval, and many people waved small U.S. flags.

Biles landed her final flip to cap off a flawless routine. When the music stopped, she had a giant smile on her face. Biles's teammates ran over and hugged her. With the help from her performance, Team USA won the gold medal in team gymnastics.

◄ **Simone Biles blew away her competition in the individual all-around.**

▲ **Team USA won gold in team gymnastics,
Russia won silver, and China won bronze.**

"It's everything I'd hoped and then some," Biles said about
competing in the Olympics.[4] The next competition for Biles was
the individual all-around. She wowed fans throughout the four
events. Biles opened with a powerful, **acrobatic** vault. She
swung smoothly on the uneven bars. Then she put together a
steady performance while linking together difficult moves on
the **balance beam**. Finally, she closed things out with another
athletic, acrobatic performance on floor exercise. By the end,
there was no doubt who had performed the best. Biles was
the gold-medal winner. She celebrated with her teammate Aly
Raisman, who finished second in the competition.

Biles became the talk of the Games as she kept winning medals. She went for her fourth medal in a floor final. Each flip earned gasps of amazement from the crowd. When she had finished her final routine of the Games, she stood up and thanked the crowd. They cheered wildly. Biles had won her fourth gold medal. At that time, only three other gymnasts had won four gold medals during one Olympics: Soviet gymnast Larisa Latynina in 1956, Věra Čáslavská of Czechoslovakia in 1968, and Romania's Ecaterina Szabo in 1984. It was all smiles for Biles and the rest of Team USA.

THINK ABOUT IT

▶ Why do you think people care about an international competition such as the Olympics?

▶ Olympic athletes put in a lot of time and energy to practice their sports. Why do you think they do this?

▶ Do you think it's important for athletes around the world to meet each other? Why or why not? What are the advantages and disadvantages?

GLOSSARY

acrobatic (ak-ruh-BAT-ik): Acrobatic means to perform skilled gymnastic moves. Biles showed her acrobatic skills.

balance beam (BAL-uhns BEEM): A balance beam is a 4-inch (10-cm) wide beam raised off the ground and is used in gymnastics. Biles did backflips on the balance beam.

consecutive (kuhn-SEK-yuh-tiv): Consecutive means it happened in a row. Gardner stopped Karelin from winning his fourth consecutive Olympic gold medal.

frame (FRAYM): The physical size or shape of a person's body is known as the person's frame. The wrestler had a large frame.

freestyle (FREE-stile): In swimming, freestyle is when racers can use any swimming stroke they want, though most use the front crawl. Phelps competed in a freestyle race.

glided (GLY-ded): Glided means to have moved in a smooth motion. The skater glided around the ice.

heavyweight (HEV-ee-wayt): Heavyweight is a term used in wrestling to signify the heaviest class of wrestlers. Karelin was considered a heavyweight.

heptathlon (hep-TATH-luhn): A competition for women in the Olympics that involves seven events: the 100-meter hurdles, high jump, shot put, 200-meter dash, long jump, javelin throw, and 800-meter run. In 1988, Joyner-Kersee competed in the heptathlon.

relay (REE-lay): A relay is a race that involves team members working together. Phelps competed in a swimming relay.

strides (STRIDES): Strides are very long steps. The runner's strides helped her win the race.

SOURCE NOTES

1. Saj Chowdhury. "London 2012: The Real Florence Griffith-Joyner." *BBC.* BBC, 5 Apr. 2012. Web. 26 Dec. 2018.

2. "Lezak Runs Down French to Win Relay Gold for U.S." *ESPN.* ESPN, 11 Aug. 2008. Web. 26 Dec. 2018.

3. Ibid.

4. "Simone Biles Creates Artistic Gymnastics History in Rio." *Olympic.* Olympic Games, 12 Sept. 2016. Web. 26 Dec. 2018.

TO LEARN MORE

BOOKS

Herman, Gail. *What Are the Summer Olympics?*
New York, NY: Grosset & Dunlap, 2016.

Mason, Tyler. *Incredible Olympic Records.*
Mankato, MN: The Child's World, 2017.

McAneney, Caitie. *Simone Biles: Greatest Gymnast of
All Time.* New York, NY: PowerKids Press, 2018.

WEBSITES

Visit our website for links about the Olympics: **childsworld.com/links**

*Note to Parents, Teachers, and Librarians: We routinely verify our Web links to make
sure they are safe and active sites. So encourage your readers to check them out!*

Biles, Simone, 27–29

Fernandez, Lisa, 20

Gardner, Rulon, 15, 17
Griffith Joyner,
    Florence, 11–13
gymnastics, 4, 27–29

heavyweight, 15
Heiden, Eric, 7–9
heptathlon, 13
home run, 20

Joyner-Kersee,
    Jackie, 13

Lezak, Jason, 24

Phelps, Michael,
    23–25
pitcher, 20

softball, 19–20
speed skating, 7–9
swimming, 4, 23–25

track and field, 4,
    11–13

wrestling, 15, 17